The Garden
WHERE ALL LOVES END

Melissa Morphew

Melissa Morphew

*To Matt,
a wonderful poet
and a great student —
it's been great
getting to
read your
poems —*

1996 WINNER:

NATIONAL POETRY BOOK SERIES

LA JOLLA POETS PRESS

*Melissa Morphew
Huntsville, TX
April 4, 2001*

ISBN: 0-931721-13-X
Library of Congress Number: 97-70019
First Edition

La Jolla

P O E T S   P R E S S

Kathleen Iddings • Editor/Publisher

P.O. Box 8638
La Jolla, CA 92038

COVER DESIGN

Patricia R. Barnett
127 Spinnaker Court, Del Mar, CA 92014

Acknowledgements

The author wishes to thank the following magazines in which some of these poems (sometimes in earlier versions) have appeared or are scheduled to appear:

ASCENT: "The Missionary Writes To Her Fiancé Concerning Poetry".
"The Missionary Writes To Her Fiancé Concerning Baptism".

NEW VIRGINIA REVIEW: "The Missionary Writes To Her Fiancé Concerning Fire".
"The Missionary Writes To Her Fiancé Concerning Martydom".
"The Missionary Writes To Her Fiance Concerning The Strength Of Women".
"The Missionary Writes To Her Fiance Concerning Innocence".

NEGATIVE CAPABILITY: "Creation".
"Elegy For Robert Icarius McKee".
"Legacy".
"All The Names Of God".

PARNASSUS: POETRY IN REVIEW: "The Missionary Writes To Her Fiancé Concerning Blindman's Bluff".

POEM: "Dusk At The 25th Annual First Baptist Picnic"
"Sitting Up With Thomas (Aged 2)".

POET LORE: "The Missionary Writes To Her Fiancé Concerning the Nature Of God".
"The Missionary Writes To Her Fiancé Concerning A Small Death".

POETRY EAST: "The Missionary Writes To Her Fiancé Concerning Hunger".
"The Missionary Writes To Her Fiancé Concerning Desire".
"Notes For A Lecture To The Art Students: Another Way To Hear".

SHENANDOAH: "Cleansed".

SOUTHERN POETRY REVIEW: "The Missionary Writes To Her Fiancé Concerning The Living And The Dead".

The poems included in the "Hunger And Heat" section of this manuscript were published as a chapbook by Anabiosis Press in December 1995.

The author also wishes to thank the Tennessee Arts Commission for a grant which helped provide time for the completion of these poems.

"The Missionary Writes To Her Fiancé Concerning Blindman's Bluff" was the winner of the 1993 Randall Jarrell International Poetry Prize sponsored by the North Carolina Writers' Network.

Finally, the author would like to thank the following people for their advice and support: Coleman Barks, Jim Clark, Judith Ortiz Cofer, Stephen Corey, Eugenie Hamner, Judson Mitcham, and Sue Brannan Walker.

Foreword

...and lucent syrops, tinct with cinnamon

What is the place of lushness in a world of fiber-optic cable, hardbodies, nuclear reactors, Wall Street computerized trading, hard drives, soft money, and so-called intimate relationships born across electronic pathways whose very existence is predicated upon the absence of physicality—the denial of touch, texture, and density? When abundance has come to be associated with the assets of the *Fortune* 500, of *Forbe*'s fifty most wealthy Americans, and of certain body parts on certain cinematic and athletic celebrities, how does one argue for wealth and surfeit of a very different kind?

Melissa Morphew's poems are no throwback to some age we might now see as more romantic and desirable (in both narrow and broad regards) than our own. Still, her work is informed by a sensibility not common at the close of the millennium, and the distinctive sound of her mind's shape rewards us with strange but satisfying takes on a world of luxuriant possibilities to which we have become generally inured. From the beginning Morphew hints at where we will be going, offering these words in "Cleansed," her opening poem: *I'm looking for the perfect / love, a raspberry briar / siphoned to the surface of a toe / with bacon fat...* And whether she is approaching family matters, religion, historical figures such as Anastasia, or poetry itself, Morphew seems repeatedly to be asking why *so many ascetics / of self-induced famine / deny the existence / of such a clotted-cream / and strawberry kind of love* as she would wish to foster in *The Garden Where All Loves End*.

The first of this book's two sections, "Garden," shows us the range of Morphew's life-hungry voices and rhythms: here we find the taut simplicity of "Sitting Up with Thomas (Aged 2)" and the tautly symbolic "Flight"; and here we also find the rollicking catalogued history of God's early life ("Creation") followed quickly by the self-conscious, almost surreal, but still wise catalogue of "Notes for a Lecture to the Art Students: Another Way to Hear." Yet the second section, "Hunger and Heat (The Missionary Letters)," is Morphew's *piece de resistance*. There, the poet's insistence on an altered worldview is rendered through the voice of a woman who, speaking to her fiancé as she does from the relative wilds of several far sides of the earth, approaches the other-worldly while still being deeply grounded.

Not by accident does Morphew offer as epigraph to "The Missionary Letters" a passage from Wallace Stevens' "Sunday Morning," with its *pungent fruit and bright* and its things of the earth *to be cherished like the thought of heaven.* Stevens' central and nearly unfathomable belief, that the human imagination literally creates and moves the world, is handmaiden here to Morphew's openhearted (but by no means innocent) sensuality, and to her defiance of a whole range of cultural norms.

In John Keats's "The Eve of St. Agnes" a myth is made real, and reality turned mythic, by young Madeline's mostly pristine faith in an old Christian-romantic legend and by young Porphyro's closeted, decidedly unpristine ardor. As the youthful female missionary of "Hunger and Heat" tries to sort out her life in a series of letters to her no-doubt frustrated and threatened lover—whose voice we never hear—we are allowed to witness a similar blending of actuality with dream, and of Stevens' exalted view of imagination with what he has termed *the pressure of reality.*

Melissa Morphew's striking poems, sometimes grim but always lovely, persistently seek that realm where the ordinary need not be settled for merely because it is in fact what we have, where loss and failure rightly perceived—and rightly spoken—become beautiful, lasting triumph:

I remembered flowers my mother grew,
fire-flame lilies:
the bees never touched the petals
but hung suspended just above—
the moment when lovers are about to kiss,
their lips haven't met,
and there's only breath.

–Stephen Corey

Stephen Corey is the author of six collections of poems, most recently *All These Lands You Call One Country.* (University of Missouri Press, 1992), and of numerous essays, critical articles, and reviews. He is the associate editor of *The Georgia Review,* where he has been on staff since 1983.

For my parents
Levi Thomas Morphew
and
Elizabeth Anne Weathers Morphew—

and for my best friend, Lorena Sins - thanks for listening.

Table of Contents

II. HUNGER AND HEAT (THE MISSIONARY LETTERS)

The Missionary Writes to Her Fiancé—

...the Garden
Where all loves end
Terminate torment
Of love unsatisfied
The greater torment
Of love satisfied
End of the endless
Journey to no end...

–T.S. Eliot, "Ash Wednesday",

I

GARDEN

Cleansed

I'm looking for the perfect
love, a raspberry briar
siphoned to the surface of a toe
with bacon fat, the relief,
the magic of old wisdom
when there is no reason
for the stone from the white deer's belly
to draw out the fever
but the forehead cools
and the evidence waits in the April water
of a rainbarrel, a thin yellow
line of pus, the remnants of the wound,
and I keep the stone to remember
because nothing marks my body,
smooth as river slate.

Creation

And God was a green lizard
sleeping on the edge of the world,
soaking-in the sun—

and this was before love,
before the visions of honeysuckle
and tangerine that would make Him
lonely, before He wished Himself
a bird, a snowy egret
caught on the wind's blade,
a wisp of grey, an early March morning,
before He knew everything
like $E=mc^2$ or which roots are edible
or how the moon affects the tides
or when to plant nasturtium,
this was before He was a girl
and the stars became tangled
in Her long dark hair
and fell into the night
with each tug of Her comb,
before He grew thistle and foxglove,
chicory and coriander, before He laughed
and waterfalls came spinning down the mountains,
this was before He was a toad
chasing a golden ball, or before He was a hag
hiding hunger in Her cloak,
long before He painted himself wind-blown yellow,
spent afternoons in a Monet meadow, walking
in silver-maple shade, before He became
pestilence and famine and urge, before He
ate six pomegranate seeds
and spit out the seasons, before He lived
as a princess with eleven sisters
who scuffed Their shoes across the deserts
every night in the whirlwind dance
of the earth, before He was a wolf
or a fingerless girl sinking to the floor

of the sea, and long before He lay down
in the field of the sky, His great stomach
split open like a gourd out of which
poured light and darkness, land and water,
hickory nuts and angel fish, mudhens
and turtles, dragonflies
and frigate birds, oysters
and coral, before He hated
the silence and had to speak,
before He learned to sing,
long before snow and rain,
before He became all possibility,
before He imagined death,
before everything—

When God was a green lizard
sleeping on the edge of the world,
dreaming. . .

The Poet Talks to her Mother's Ghost About the Symbolism of Dreams

Mama,

Have you ever had a dream
where you made love to a stranger?
Your fingers coveting
the golden-red hairs of his chest.
Around his neck a thin silver chain
shimmers with constellations.

He takes you to a place of water—
the Euphrates, or the Congo, or the Amazon—
gives you a cobalt feather
snatched from a wayward macaw.
The feather becomes a silk scarf,
and he ties your hands behind your back
with an intricate lovers' knot,
kisses the lobe of your ear.

You are dressed in a Seurat watercolor,
tiny dots flash like mica in the sun.
The stranger whispers
"lamplight, coral, meteor, bone"
You answer
"leafmold, trilobite, opal, fern"

He sets you free.
Together you swim down
the emerald-black river,
breathing water like air.

Notes for a Lecture to the Art Students: Another Way to Hear

1. Trust your eyes—
   tree roots
   might be a man's hands
   knobby with age.
   A toadstool
   a woman's face
   streaked with tears.

2. We know clouds
   have all sorts of guises,
   but the best of you
   will catch them
   in transformation—
   a halibut changing to a hare,
   a locomotive dissolving
   to mist on the lake.

3. Most people look like
   frogs or dogs or fishes.

4. Remember everything
   is simply a shape
   in relation to another shape
   with a distance between.

5. It's obvious God thought in circles
   and triangles and squares.

6. Touch the canvas; leave fingerprints.

7. It does not matter
   how many angels dance
   on the head of a pin
   but how many sleep
   beneath the curve
   of your eyelid.

8. Ten in one million people
   taste in color.

9. There are black butterflies
   which weave the sky
   like ash from a volcano.

10. Clean your brushes
    with linseed oil and turpentine.

11. In a French museum
    behind a glass screen,
    a dried peach
    bears the label
    "Van Gogh's Ear."

Dusk at the 25th Annual First Baptist Picnic

Church virgins
know little of love,
bob on light
between bright checkered squares,
green wicker baskets,
plates emptied of fried chicken
and the half-moons of fried-apple pies.
Babies feel the pull of nursery-rhyme stars.
Their mothers hum softly,
promise dreams of a beautiful shore.

He sees her
scattering crumbs beneath the trees,
supper for late-going birds,
like bits of prayers
memorized in Sunday school
but then forgotten—
On the fourth day
God made the sun.
On the sixth day
He made Adam.
Eve was born
from an innocence of bone—
A breeze snags her hem,
flutters pink gauze.

To Feel the Eggshell

The first time my heart was broken
Mama handed me a dustpan and a broom.
Then she told me this story:

  My great-aunt Ophelia had two children.
  One day the little ones followed a cloud
  of lavender butterflies into the woods,
  enticed by the wind-chime flutter of wings.

  By suppertime they hadn't come home.
  Ophelia called and called. But no answer,
  only the silence of early lightning bugs, glowing
  green-gold in the branches of the pear trees.

  Late that evening, she and Uncle Benny
  finally found their babies, arms and legs akimbo
  like sleeping rag dolls, face down
  in a patch of deadly nightshade—
  their mouths full of blackish berries,
  their fingers grubby with purple juice.

  And burdened by the weight of her name,
  what could Ophelia do but go crazy?
  Benny caught her wandering their garden
  in her pink flannel gown, clutching a turnip,
  mumbling Italian sonnets to the arch-angel Gabriel.

  He hated to do it, but Uncle Benny
  sent her to the state sanitarium.
  He cried when the doctors took her away,
  sprinkled his overalls with her lemon verbena,
  wore her aprons while he plowed.

  The doctors put Ophelia to work washing dishes,
  great stacks of heavy green-rimmed plates.
  She scrubbed for four weeks straight,
  night and day, chanting strange prayers:

"Dear God, thank you
for the blue delphinium,
the long-handled rake.
It's good to feel the eggshell
crack against the bowl.
Bless the mole and the weevil.
Let us have fennel-seed cake for dinner.
The world is weary with the smell of mothballs."

The doctors took her for a hopeless case.
Told Benny breaking the spell of a mother's grief
was more difficult than catching moonlight in a jelly jar.

But one morning, the kitchen sweet
with the scent of mock orange,
Ophelia stared hard out the open window
and told the nurse standing guard:
"I'm tired of washing dishes.
If you let me go home,
I promise I won't be crazy."

Ophelia had another baby,
a little girl born with puckered fingers.
She named her Belladonna.
Rocked her to sleep every night humming
"Au Claire de la Lune."

The Girl who Attempted Suicide Tries to Explain

My parents tell me I dreamed Jesus.
He was nothing more
than the luminous glow
of the clock beside my bed.

"Do not believe in angels," they said.
But I never told them I did.

I wanted to suffer some annunciation.
To become a flower or a bird.

And so what if it's blasphemy?

I shook out my dress in the wind,
stood naked, a lotus
resting on green water—
an empty china cup.

Jesus asked me if I believed
mornings could be like linen,
sweet with the smell of a new bar of soap?

I said yes. Walked out
into March sun blustered
with cloud.

The sky hurt me—
a swallowtail wing
leeched colorless
                    in flight.

Prodigal

[for my brother Stephen in a coma 8 years]

He left home
2 p.m. on a Wednesday
clouds threatening storm,
a pleasant ominousness,
loamy scent of pine and mosses,
and the road flat to the horizon
then dipping behind a hill.
He always thought he could return
but even one mile is not so simple.
And if he could tell you about his life
balled up in his fist, too tight,
his pockets full of baubles—a plastic pin
shaped like Florida, chewing gum foil
folded into origami swans—you'd understand
how when he opens his hand, its empty
and the way of everything is loss, entropy, each day
bits going down the drain, sucked up the vacuum,
the universe devouring itself,
black holes and quasars, and this writing
will deconstruct like the *Mission Impossible* tape,
an impossible mission, the prodigal
who lost the map his father said
keep close to the heart, but that night
a sandstorm in the desert took his compass,
his cloak, and every night since
there have been no stars.

Zelda: 1948

I want God
to put his thumbprint
on my forehead, say yes
you are as real
as delphinium in the garden.

Lately, I can feel
the earth's axis shift,
and I lose my footing,
float like Chagall's kiss
in cabbage-moth rapture.

I wear white lace dresses.
People mistake me for an angel,
ask me to cure their wounds,
find the loves that slipped away
like summer kites.

When I was ten, my mother
taught me to skin-a-cat—
hang upside down, the blood pounding
in my head, swing and flip,
land.

But now, I'm a high wire act
where there's nothing
to hold onto.
I jump

through hoops of fire—
my hair catches, golden filaments
burning out like a sparkler
while I fall,

and God refuses
to transform me
into lupine or asphodel
or salt.

The Fat Woman
Falls in Love with her Body

Or does she?
Is this possible?
Mornings in the shower
as her hands glide across
the protuberance of her belly,
does she remember
the soft sweet bread she's eaten
and think—
This is good?
Does she admire
the creamy mallow of her breasts,
the toffee-colored aureoles?
Does she praise
the folds of flesh,
her sturdy thighs,
a walking genoise,
the sweat of her skin
trailing the vague scent
of caramel-almond nougat?
When so many ascetics
of self-induced famine
deny the existence
of such a clotted-cream
and strawberry kind of love,
a love of chocolate dipped abundance,
free from the confines
of girdles, accepting of flaws,
can she truly be happy
with the feast
of her body?

Leaving The Labyrinth

At night while I'm sleeping, I'm building wings
not in my dreams, but sleepwalking;
when I wake I find the feathers
scattered throughout the house—
titmouse and moorhen behind the couch,
in the cupboards, oriole and lapwing.
I vacuum, but every morning there are more—
marbled murrelet and Carolina wren,
red-throated pipit and yellow-eyed junco
poking from beneath pillows,
marking the pages of my books.

But I can't find the wings—
I've looked in the closets, the attic,
the basement-dark corners full of spiders and dust.
I'm good at keeping secrets, even from myself.
Where can they be? And what do they look like?
A tufted pinata? A motley angel shimmering
the tealight-amethyst of African hummingbirds,
the subtle cornflower of mountain jays?

And one morning, will I wake
to find myself gone, flown to Marakesh or Bangkok
or somewhere even further,
clothed in the plumage of egrets and kestrels,
the bright feathers of osprey and flamingoes
embroidered to my skin.

Anastasia

How they worry over my bones—
As if anyone could survive
such atrocity—as if I could have been
an old woman in Virginia
married to a man with a hapless crew cut,
slavishly tending hundreds of cats—

They are wild with the dream
of me—they secretly need
a fairytale princess rescued from the death pit,
scarred by bayonets, but breathing—
And suddenly I become one of them,
a victim, a commoner,

no longer the little girl
who strolled along the snow-crusted Neva
warm in her seal skin coat,
no longer the pampered daughter
whose father gave her gold and emerald
eggs for Easter, the one who ate chocolates
from Switzerland while the peasants starved—

How easily hate turns to love—
They make me a martyr
because I was young,
as if youth equals innocence,
as if I hadn't spent my last days
pining for the Winter Palace
planning my escape
back into the crystal snow

of my old life, stubbornly sure
princesses cannot die
before they have been
properly kissed.

Ars Poetica

Sunporch-blue summer,
105^0,
a yellow dress
slung across the back of a chair.
She sleeps
in panties and bra;
the ceiling fan clicks
a small litany of wind,
moves the chimes—
a silver sound she hears
as dreams of water.
She is waiting for a lover,
the man who will bring
a bouquet of gladiolia
and his mother's ring.
He is late, as usual.
When he arrives,
he finds her
on a chintz sofa handpainted
with lemon-colored roses.
Her skin a fever, he draws his finger
down each vertebra, but still
she does not wake.
He scatters the gladiolia petals,
then departs
without the requisite kiss—
learning none of her secrets,
but happy
in a way he cannot name.

Legacy

Eve's garden sprouts broken Wedgewood,
bits of Dresden, handles of demitasse cups—
the shards gleam beneath the trillium
as Eve weeds and hoes,
burying the umber virility of hyacinth bulbs.

She doesn't question the china's existence.
She assumes the porcelain spines
to be deathtraps for errant slugs,
hidden there by a cross-eyed angel
on the first day of the world.

          Only creatures
the angel could see from his right eye
were deemed beautiful.
The rest became a bane to God.
A sadness in Eve's heart
divines how this skewed gaze
will fall on her sons.

She creeps from her bed at midnight
lost in the thought of stars—
Adam named the constellations
after monsters and princesses,
but she would have called them
lily and violet, aster and chrysanthemum.

Eve wishes she had daughters;
with girls, she might dig up the china,
piece together a set of plates,
an heirloom proper for a bottom drawer.

She would teach her daughters the difference
between toadstools and mushrooms,
show them the blackberry bushes
growing wild by the river,
warn them the sweetest fruit lies
tangled with briars in unpredictable dark.

Sitting up with Thomas (Aged 2)

Yes, and I spread my fingers
to admire their length
and marvel at my own simplicity,
the pale skin. My nail's thin opaque shimmer,
somehow like water,
somehow like the milk-fire of opal.
And I know there is beauty
in holding a pencil,
in holding a spoon,
in taking the head of a dandelion
between thumb and index,
snapping the stem.
Grace flows with the movement of a needle,
the spinning of colored thread.
And love touches a brow
to know the depth of fever,
smoothing the hair back,
smoothing the hair.

Elegy for Robert Icarius McKee

My father grew grapes,
the lush vines twining around cheap chicken wire.
Summer mornings, I would help him
pick the purple-blue fruit.
Sometimes the husks split open
from ripeness, exposing green flesh
pale as mucus.
Daddy knew their names—
Buffalo, Dulcet, Tarheel, Alden.
He'd whisper them, the way devout men
might say the twenty-third psalm.
And he'd make wine,
wine so sweet it needed to be drunk
more than once a year at communion
when starched white ladies
peeled off their stockings, and for humility,
washed each other's feet.
But then the wine soured.
Daddy began to chart the movement of stars.
He'd stagger home singing
"Amazing grace, how sweet the sound
that saved a wretch like me. . ."
off-key, solemn.
I remember times
I found Mama
crying quietly in the bathroom.
And one night,
when there wasn't any moon,
she took the pruning shears,
cut down vine after vine.

Visions of Women

Some say we are small
with the bones of birds
or rodents,
nibbling crumbs beneath the shade
of dahlias, columbine, larkspur. . .
Any gardener's herbal
recounts the dreams—
the Virgin Mary as damask rose,
the Magdalene as black narcissus.
We have been gilded with iridescence,
pressed dry between pages
of dusty books, preserved under glass,
the minutiae of our wings thought
too bright a blue, a color
too strange to exist,
the color of flight
and water.

Folklore

It's that familiar story—
only it's true this time,
mostly because it happened in Mexico,
far enough away.

On the dark of the moon,
a girl grows desperate enough,
lonely enough,
to have sex with her dog,
a mangy alley mutt with yellow fur.
And nine months later she gives birth
to a litter of puppies with human faces.

She does this in secret, alone.
And in the same way—
because she's a good Catholic
and it's plain the priest can't come—
she christens them with stolen holy water:
Jésus, José, Gabriel, Maria.

But you know how it goes.
The townspeople find out,
the village elders storm her house,
pulling the runt Gabriel away from her breast,
and taking the yelping things
down to the river.
Their eyes weren't even opened.

And the girl, who had followed
screaming *"por favor, por favor, por favor,"*
goes crazy with grief,

slashes the men with her fingernails,
bites them hard enough to bring blood.

So the head man, known for being wise,
has the others tie her down, gag her.
They'll teach her
what it's like to be with a man.
Maybe this will cure her.

But when they're done,
their semen still wet and sticky on her thighs,
something in her face tells him he's wrong,
and he kicks her bound body into the river.

To the Boy in the Navy Peacoat on the 3rd Floor of the University Library

Hey you with the x-ray vision,
boy with neon-blue eyes,
did you notice anything unusual under my sweater,
once you'd stripped me down to my panties and bra?
Did you see how patches of my skin glisten with scales,
shimmer like sequins on Nina Simone's gown?
Yeah, well, I moonlight as a mermaid
singing the blues five fathoms deep,
swimming the reef with a couple of dusky damselfish
and one mean son-of-a-bitch nassau grouper.
And you better believe I can take you down,
but you just might get lost in the rare rose coral,
the brittle passages of fire—*millepora complanata,*
porites furcata, madracis mirbilis, acropora palmata—
I'm into the spell of words,
equally adept with magic on land or at sea,
but all those sailors drowned because they wanted to.
I have no power over fate.
So, hey, think twice before you begin this fairytale
about what it means
to find your dream girl.

The Water's Edge

You see it makes a better story
if it was April,
the riverbank a haze of tentative green.
But to tell the truth,
I don't remember—
so I could say
it was like traveling outside my body
or like larkspur in sudden wind,
and it wouldn't be a lie—
and I might tell you
of an elderly aunt dressed in purple,
her face a dried kumquat
beneath the wide brim of a black straw hat—
she would be the one
to write my name down in the Family Bible,
her knotted fingers inking in the date—
and I did have such an aunt,
though she was dead
by the time I felt the touch
of the preacher's hand,
the white linen handkerchief
covering my nose and mouth—
but you will imagine her singing anyway,
a little off key, surrounded
by her sisters in grace, so close
to the water's edge, the river
licked the tips of their patent leather shoes—
and that's how it could have been,
and probably was—
spring, my parents and grandparents
looking on, behind them an open meadow,
a patch of yellow jonquils where a house once stood,
and my feet sinking into soft mud,
the preacher leading me on,
crossing the algae-slick stones
until the water was waist deep,
and he cupped me in the curve of his arms,

held me beneath the murky water
just long enough to embrace
the love of Jesus—
I'm almost sure
that's how it was.

Flight

The monarch caterpillar, like I love you,
strains against a chrysallis, dreaming
intently each night of angel wings,
fearing the sycamore shade burning
blue-green in paper-lanterned twilight,
knowing his instinct will drive him
south toward Mexico, his heart beating,
and he will breathe without thinking,
navigating some secret map ancient
as the rivers of Mars,
avoiding at all costs
a human touch, the brush
of yellow dust from his body.

All the Names of God

"There is said to be a group of Buddhist monks in Tibet
compiling all the names of God; when they are finished, the
world is to end."

—from *Language and the Sexes*

They travel the knotted cartography
of this world in their orange robes,
bare heads blistered by the wind,
asking everywhere they go
"What is the name of God?"

Some are easy—Osiris, Yahweh, Krishna—
but others are buried deep, so they dig
for broken stones, and like blind men
let the words seep into their fingers.

Their voluminous pens never register surprise.
In a grass hut in Kenya, Pope John Paul
and Elvis grace a wall side by side.

A man in Poughkeepsie answers, "Burma Shave."
A woman in Paris hordes a box of abalone shell buttons.
She uses them to explain the way horses graze
in soft white fog.

A young New Zealander, nursing a collicky child,
adds chrysanthemum and sitar, her mouth
holding each syllable like lemon candy,
the bite of chinquapin, water spout, dust.

The monks trudge on.
A thousand consonants stain their tongues,
so they pray for an end, a word
like chocolate melting in noonday sun,
but still the list grows—carbon 14 and hyperspace theory,
holstein cows, Modigliani, sunflower seeds,
sludge. . .

Postcards from Weldon Kees

1.
Argentina's not as full of Nazis
as you'd think.

Dark women sit on white balconies
brushing their hair—
exquisite black orchids in moonlight.

No one would ever dream to die
for poetry.

2.
Desire is stupid,
but I've forgotten why.

Two hours on the beach
doused in coconut oil,
sipping a Long Island tea,
I watched a sailboat
make its way to the horizon,
propelled by the invisible.

3.
Walking in the hills,
I came upon the ruin of a church,
small turquoise birds
perched on crumbling ochre walls.

I thought of God's logic—
how he made me in his image.

All I did was close my eyes,
stick a pin in a map,
and this is how it ended.

Notes Toward a Novel
That Will Never Be Finished

Chapter One:

Nothing much happens.
Dandelions grow wild
in a yard on the edge of town.
An old man in grey coveralls
(Let's call him Sam?)
picks them, puts them in a clay crock,
adds sugar and yeast,
months fermenting in the heat
(this is the South, maybe Texas?)—
his wine the sweetest in the county,
but no one will drink it—
the community dry as a Baptist.
(Sam?) goes to the July Revival Meeting,
spikes the iced tea—
all the women of the Ladies' Auxiliary
become tipsy, dancing amongst tombstones,
twirling the skirts of their polyester dresses,
flapping their arms in angelic dementia.
The oldest (Mrs. Gabriel?) (or is that too cute?)
climbs the stairs of the bell tower,
perches on a cornice
(she should be at least 90-95
with black, black eyes
but surprisingly few wrinkles).
Everyone below is screaming hysterically—
they all know she has terminal cancer
and of course the conclusion—suicide.
(Mrs. Michael?) (maybe that's better,
less obvious) looks down at the crowd,
begins singing (not "Amazing Grace"
too cliche, perhaps an old
Billie Holiday standard, something bluesy).
She's up there a full three minutes,

but she doesn't jump, nor is she raptured
by moths or butterflies or crows,
she simply climbs down,
by which point
everyone is sober.

Chapter Two:

Is totally unrelated to Chapter One
(having concluded fictive connections
often seem overly contrived)
except that it takes place
in (Sam's?) memory—
He is on a train with (his mother?
father? maiden aunt?).
It's during the Depression,
they're leaving the city
because food is scarce
(in this instance perhaps his maiden aunt
works best—but he's not an orphan,
no, his parents simply had to stay
for some valid reason,
something that would justify
separation from a child,
maybe they both have TB—
after all it's highly contagious).
(Sam?) looks out the window,
the fields pass frame by frame like a film.
He and his aunt are on their way
to his grandparent's farm
in the (Tennessee?) hills.
It will be the first time
he's seen a cow (an opportunity
for comic relief). The family
becomes embroiled in a murder case.
The aunt (Marci?) is raped, then strangled.
The case is never solved.

(Sam?) suffers no traumatic effects,
and (in an avoidance
of traditional plot lines)
has no desire in years to come
to track down her killer.

Chapters 3-20:

Will be worked out
in detail later,
but pivotal scenes should involve
(Sam's?) years in the circus (as a peanut vendor?
trapeze artist? rodeo clown?),
the purchase of a green parakeet named (Edgar?),
a love affair gone sour with a (school teacher?
trapeze artist? waitress?) named (Edna?)
whose long dark hair reminds him
of a river.

Epilogue:

Finally the beginning
has a connection with the end.
It is (Mrs. Gabriel's? Michael's?) funeral.
(Sam?) doesn't go,
but is in town to buy two-penny nails.
His dog (Tambourine?) comes with him.
They walk by the hearse
parked in front of (Taylor's?) funeral home.
(Sam?) kicks the right rear tire,
(Tambourine?) sniffs it.
Ending with the image
of dog and man continuing
down the road. (Of course
all this is tentative.)

Time has no meaning, space and place have no meaning, on this
journey. All times can be inhabited, all places visited. In
a single day the mind can make a millpond of the oceans. Some
people who have never crossed the land they were born on have
travelled all over the world—

Jeanette Winterson, *Sexing the Cherry*

Shall she not find in comforts of the sun,
In pungent fruit and bright, green wings, or else
In any balm or beauty of the earth,
Things to be cherished like the thought of heaven?—

Wallace Stevens, "Sunday Morning"

II

HUNGER & HEAT
The Missionary Letters

The Missionary Writes to her Fiancé Concerning Hunger

Dear David,

This lost continent
teems with parrots and teacups.
The heat overpowers me.
I brought six white linen dresses
and a parasol to match,
one lovely ball gown of emerald satin—
in the moonlight it appears black.
Young men ask me to dance
and we move slowly
like lilies on still water.
Hands stroke my shoulders,
whisper—"how beautiful, how pale."
The air is delicious with vanilla—
it makes me hungry.
I eat and eat.
I grow fat on sesame seeds and ginger.
If you were to kiss me now,
my mouth would taste of tangerine.

The Missionary Writes to her Fiancé Concerning Blindman's Bluff

Dear David,

    On the night I was conceived,
father led mother to the garden, blindfolded.
She spun round and round, losing gravity,
orbiting father like the twisted braids of Saturn's rings.
    Finally his laugh drew her,
and they fell together into a bed of trillium.
Mother still couldn't see—her fingers
reading the braille of father's body;
each rib, each vertebra, told this story—
a sky half-covered by storm clouds,
lightning in the distance,
flowers moon-leeched to shades of darkest blue.
    Father's kisses became tangled
with the smell of mint and moonflower and lily.
They made mother feel
as if she had swallowed a hummingbird,
a luna moth, four rose petals,
and a thorn.

The Missionary Writes to her Fiancé Concerning the Straight and Narrow

Dear David,

What if God were a quantum physicist?
Then we'd be together now
but at the same time
we've never met.
And none of it
because we were good or bad,
just the random dance
of milkweed caught in wind.
        And everything's true
and everything's false
all at once; time
is and is not,
every place is some place else,
we are everyone
and no one at all.
How wonderful to embrace existence
simultaneously.
And isn't that
the definition of omniscience?

The Missionary Writes to her Fiancé Concerning the Living and the Dead

Dear David,

   November 2 was the Day of the Dead.
Father Felipé headed a procession
for Saint Guillermo of the Mirthful Tears
whose body was carried by the faithful
in a boxed-in chair with a window,
his face pressed against the glass,
staring squint-eyed at the crowd
from folds of dusty wrinkles.
And it did seem as if he were laughing,
sharing some private joke
with God about heaven.

   Young girls in white trailed behind,
carrying yellow calendulas
bright as Aztec suns; they would skip and run,
occasionally dropping a flower in the dust.
When they reached the cemetery,
picnic cloths were spread on the ground.
The villagers ate round loaves of bread
decorated with sugar skulls, their honeyed grins
like the dark trick of a possum.

   All through the last days of October
death has been with us, shaped in candy and candles,
piled high with fruits and flowers,
sung softly in songs which drift
with the lake's slow ripple
out across the water,
saying welcome, welcome,
you are not alone.

The Missionary Writes to her Fiancé Concerning Innocence

Dear David,

Summers in the garden,
my cousin Isabel and I
played hide-and-seek
among eternities of bean-row
weighted with morning glory vines,
purple flowers closed in late evening dusk.

She taught me to waltz,
dancing in our petticoats, white
apparitions under the moon.

Chasing fireflies,
we made japanese lanterns out of mason jars,
their bronze lids riddled with holes.

Isabel had a bottom drawer lined
with wedding gown lace;
she said it was full of things
we all need—baby clothes and china cups.

In the quiet of the cornstalks
chewing raw green beans,
she told me our destiny was to marry,
to let a man enter our bodies.

"He'll touch you here," she said
her pale fingers between my legs,
warming the starched cotton center
of my panties.

She kissed me on the mouth.
Her skin smelled of new dirt
and the bitter yellow of tomato blooms.

The Missionary Writes to her Fiancé Concerning Fruit and Ignorance

Dear David,

An orange tree blooms by the window. I wake
each morning to its sugary smell.
For breakfast I eat
kumquats, dates, and lemons, brought
by my African friend, Marie-Claire.
She, herself, resembles a fig,
her brown stomach rounded,
heavy with child.
              She came to the mission
seeking salvation.
She says the father is a white man,
a preacher.
              "He say Marie-Claire a bad girl,
evil, because I suck his cock
and enjoy it.
But he ask me to, miss—
I do not understand.
Will I go to hell?
His cock is tattooed with a cross.
It fill me up, so I feel satisfied.
I promise I will love this child.
I don't care she's a bastard."

We discuss names.
She likes Eva for a girl.

The Missionary Writes to her Fiancé Concerning Denial of the Flesh

Dear David,

Sundown on Good Friday,
I watched thirteen *penitentes*
descend the hill into the valley,
wearing black loin cloths,
exposing the skeletal thinness
of their shoulders and chests,
scarred from years of beatings,
nights sleeping on beds of jagged glass
and the porcelain bite of oyster shells.
They wore burlap hoods
to hide their faces,
carried cacti upon their backs,
arms stretched wide, human crosses
holding fat yellow candles
which seared dripping wax
into their palms.
Someone played the *pito*, a reed flute
whose raspy wail
rose above the drone of cicadas,
as the brothers swayed in their dance,
a dark chorus line
braiding a path through the Joshua trees.
When they reached the *Calvario*
on the eastern hillside,
one was chosen, and his brothers
nailed him to a cross—
he hung for three hours,
a living effigy
crowned by a hawthorne wreath.
The others chanted—
*"Por el castro de la sangre
Que Jesu Cristo derrama"*—
faster and faster, voices rising,

lashing themselves and the chosen one
with strips of yucca,
until they fell to their knees
kissing the ground,
moaning *"Dios. Dios."*— their bodies
spent and sweaty.

The Missionary Writes to her Fiancé Concerning the Fall

Dear David,

    I was thinking about those Sundays
one revival-hot July,
when you were teaching me to drive,
coaxing me down the back roads
of your Daddy's farm.
    We parked the truck at Chisolm Spring,
racing for the water,
leaving the stiffness of our church clothes behind.
    We dove, swinging from ropey muscadine vines
like Tarzan, reckless bodies snagging the air
so my hair fanned out in auburn wings.
    We'd eddy side by side
not touching, but so close I could see
the dark brown star that marks your eyes,
and I knew
what the angels must have felt
falling headlong from heaven.

The Missionary Writes to her Fiancé Concerning Aphrodisiacs

Dear David,

I'm reading a story
about a Persian Princess
whose husband died
impaled upon an enemy sword.
Her heart became a tongueless bird.
She did not sleep.
She could only eat the jeweled membrane
of pomegranate seeds
and the white roots of cyclamen.

The Prince's foot soldiers
brought him home.
The Princess cleaned his body
with buttermilk and yellow amaranth.
She thought "if I kiss him
he will breathe"
but she never touched lips so cold.

Her grandmother had given her a recipe—
a philtre to increase his love.

The day the Princess buried her husband,
she ripped his battle tunic to tiny bits,
steeped the rags in a jar of rosewater
with cardamon, cinnamon, and cloves.

Her grandmother told her "the husband
who drinks this potion
will satisfy his wife's every need."

The Princess drank.
The concoction had a salty edge—
blood and sweat—
she'd tasted both before.

The Missionary Writes to her Fiancé Concerning a Small Death

Dear David,

It's become my habit
to nap in the afternoons—
the heat an absinthe dew
to whet my skin.

Is this what death is?
An inertia of peace,
no breeze,
and the shadows of palm fronds.

I imagine my bones
picked clean by cloud-white cockatiels,
weightless—a feeling of evensong
when I take off my clothes
and lie down
looking out the window
at the rising moon,
stroking the secret place
behind my knees.

The cicada hum of angels
enfolds me.
An overhead fan whirs
with the motion of their wings.

The Missionary Writes to her Fiancé Concerning the Strength of Women

Dear David,

For days the snow falls
persistent as a hungry child.
Hunting is bad;
it's as if the seal never existed
and the whale with her.
The Inuit women think Sea Woman is angry.
I ask them to explain—
          In a time faraway
a daughter refused to marry,
so her father carried her
in his boat, planning
to throw her overboard,
but she didn't go easily, she held on,
forcing her father to chop
her fingers off one by one,
and each finger joint,
seduced by the magic of its own blood,
became the animals of water,
whales, seals, walrus, otter—
everything comes from her,
everything people love and fear,
food and clothes and hunger.
          And the fingerless girl
was transformed as she swirled
in the aqua eddies, sinking
to the floor of the sea.
She grew large and powerful.
Queen of the minion she created.
She built a home
of mollusk shell and fish-spine.
The wax of her candles melting
into a tallow of flesh
where the souls of slaughtered animals

come to be reborn,
pushed from the dark tunnel of her hair
back into the waves.

    And she, alone, chooses the time
to release them.

The Missionary Writes to her Fiancé Concerning the Nature of God

Dear David,

Sometimes it's impossible
to translate the word of God.
I open my hands
to show his boundless love,
and the women smile and nod
but do not understand.
    With the children it's no easier.
They listen to the story of Noah and the Flood
then chirp like monkeys for hours in the sun,
walking two by two into my house.
One little girl
with eyes brown as a last swallow of coffee,
pointed to my painting of Jesus
and said "Papa."
"No," I told her, "that is God's son."
Putting her hand over her mouth
she giggled and ran away.
    In Sunday school, I read the story
of the loaves and the fishes.
Yesterday, two little boys
brought me a slice of bread and a sardine.
"Feed our family please, Miss,
ask your God to make the magic."
It does no good to tell them
God's ways remain mysterious,
miracles grow smaller.

The Missionary Writes to her Fiancé Concerning Fire

Dear David,

I overhear tales of suttee,
women throwing themselves
on their husbands' funeral pyres.
The old ones remember.
The reverend's daughter,
a girl of nine,
asks, "How did it smell?
Did the wives scream?"
I'm horrified by the questions,
but I want to know the answers
just as much as she.
　　　　　My dreams grow worse.
It is always dawn,
the sky lighter along the horizon,
the tiny color of a bird's tongue.
I wait in the desert
wearing a white sari
trimmed with pearls and coral beads.
I can see no one,
nothing, for miles.
A shadow wheels over me,
and you descend on a pair
of enormous fawn-brown wings.
You lift me in your arms and we fly.
The sun has risen, fixed itself in the center of the sky.
Your wings beat faster without sound,
racing toward the heat.

The Missionary Writes to her Fiancé Concerning the Dangers of the Flesh and of the Silver Screen

Dear David,

    I miss the movies— the buttery dark tainted
with a smell of Old Spice, Jungle Gardenia, and warm skin,
our bodies magnetized, defeating awkward seats,
exchanging French kisses
laced with melted chocolate and mint.

    Lying here in this foreign heat,
willing myself to sleep,
I remember Gidget
in one of a hundred surfing scenes.
She almost drowns, but Moon Doggie saves her.

    What was she thinking
as the kelp tentacled her calf
and she struggled,
the surface a sunlit sheet of isinglass
she could almost touch.
Was she afraid she'd die a virgin?
Never wear his college pin?

    Moon Doggie gives her mouth to mouth.
I can tell by the way her face softens,
wobbles slightly out of focus
then fills the screen,
she will be forced to live
happily ever after.

The Missionary Writes to her Fiancé Concerning Cleanliness

Dear David,

My razor rusted.
I no longer shave
beneath my arms, I do not
scrape stiff black hairs
from my legs' pale skin. More and more
I'm the creature God made me.
In this heat, I give off
an oily fragrance of unbaked bread.
Sweat stains my blouse,
dark as the moon's eclipse.
It's all right to be a woman here.
The way a flower is a flower.

The Missionary Writes to her Fiancé Concerning Martyrdom

Dear David,

I think of the cross,
the sensation
of a nail through my hand;
Jesus was a man afterall
as well as God.
I don't have that sort of faith.
I never concentrate on sermons.
I know it's wicked
but I conjure images of myself
walking through poppy fields,
the wind necromancing the flowers,
so a million scarlet butterflies
hover the weeds.
Most times you are with me.
We walk for miles and miles
until the sweat inches down my back,
between my breasts.
I pick some flowers
and put them in your hair.

The Missionary Writes to her Fiancé Concerning Poetry

Dear David,

They jail poets here.
Take away their paper and pens,
but nothing can stop the frenzied scribbling.
One scratches her poems onto a bar of soap,
another braids them into her auburn hair.

The guards built special cells
to keep the poets away from the other prisoners,
because their walls sprout flowers,
bougainvillea, clematis, honeysuckle
cascading to the floor;
cockatoos glide
through the bars on the windows,
and no one can sleep
for the noise of crows.

One poet made friends with the moon,
hid its white light beneath her bed.
The guards threaten her with torture,
refuse to give her water and bread,
but she won't surrender the moon
and our nights are lit by stars alone,
except when there is lightning.

In the adjoining cell
a poet witched herself,
became a crabapple tree,
the tight pink buds of her fingers
opening on the last day of Mardi Gras.
In autumn, she bears fruit,
tiny alizarin apples that litter her floor.

The guards have no choice
but to eat them.

The Missionary Writes to her Fiancé Concerning Baptism

Dear David,

Every day an old man washes himself
in the yellow water
of the Ganges.
I don't mean to,
but I watch.
    His hands, sand-paper brown,
begin with his face
and he's not gentle,
a man with secrets—
a mistress his dead wife
thought would be a trick of sound,
a bell struck by wind
without volition
(but she was wrong);
or maybe he stole bread;
or worse, he was hungry
and did nothing.
    He scrubs his arms,
his chest, so fierce
he leaves scratches.
Next his legs, his feet,
still without mercy,
coating himself with the river's
thin saffron film.
    Finally modesty
forces me to turn,
but not before I share
his one tenderness—
how he holds his scrotum,
reedy fingers
barely touching the skin.
    I think of hyacinth bulbs,
a dark flower
blooming in the cup of his hands.

The Missionary Writes to her Fiancé Concerning the Dance

Dear David,

When I learned to waltz,
I imagined the body's flow
like lights upon water,
the way in China when someone dies
they set candles adrift on the river,
golden flickers, point and counter-point
of iridescent fish.

I remembered flowers my mother grew,
fire-flame lilies;
the bees never touched the petals
but hung suspended just above—
the moment when lovers are about to kiss,
their lips haven't met,
and there's only breath.

The Missionary Writes to her Fiancé Concerning Men and Angels

Dear David,

One of the older women, Clara,
swears she talks to angels.
She's been here sixteen years
and the sun has carved angles
into her face. She spends
hours in the garden hoeing red petunia beds.

She tells me,
"Michael's voice is a rusty brass bell."
He's the only famous one,
the others are cherubim, seraphim, the lower hosts.

Not everyone can hear.
A non-believer would think
she was listening to the clink of a teacup,
or the miniscule sound of needle and thread
pulled through heavy cloth.

Clara carries on the conversation
like a prayer, and she is the first to admit
angels' answers are seldom clear.

"Once," she said, " I asked them
if I should go home and marry.
Michael replied 'balsam and mugwort.'
So I planted both in my garden and stayed,
though sometimes, it's lonely here."

The Missionary Writes to her Fiancé Concerning Desire

Dear David,

Not far from the mission
Buddha rests in the jungle,
so large I could fit into his navel.
I came upon him suddenly
walking by myself
in the late afternoon.
Several monks draped in orange cloth
knelt before his altar,
strewing it with gardenias and lilies.
Burning jasmine thickened the air.
            My first impulse
was to strip off my clothes—
scale his legs, his arms,
and like a child
slide back down his belly.
I wanted to feel the cool stone
against my nakedness.

The Missionary Writes to her Fiancé Concerning the Mercy of God

Dear David,

Easter Sunday: we dyed eggs for the children,
the kitchen boiling over with the smell of vinegar,
the tips of my fingers stained
purple and blue and green—
like the feathers of a bird I saw in Mexico.

Here the birds are grey,
mockingbirds and finches
who blend into the mountain stripped
bare of trees by a crazy hunger
which eats the earth and the men
who crawl inside it.

Poverty touches everything—
the smell of polecat
faint on the edge of a yard.

They don't understand beauty;
not one child saved
an egg to look at or to hold,
as soon as they found them,
all our hard work, the delicate colors,
the intricate designs drawn carefully
with pink and yellow crayons,
was peeled, devoured whole.

The Missionary Writes to her Fiancé Concerning Distance

Dear David,

      The summer I turned five
Father left us for Paraguay.
Mother washed sheets and pillowcases,
dragged our mattresses outside
to air in the sun.
      We drank tall glasses of lemonade.
Mother smelled like lye and lemons,
her hands a raw redness
which could not heal.
      When I caught an August fever,
her touch grazed me,
too rough to smooth my pain.
Even now she apologizes—
      "I didn't know
            I was hurting."

      Spring has come.
Rain bends the flowers growing wild on the hillside.
Yesterday, I picked a bouquet of hyacinths
tattooed with small lavender bruises.
      No one will notice
from far enough away.

The Missionary Writes to her Fiancé Concerning the Rapture

Dear David,

The first boy I loved ate paste,
would stick straight pins
beneath the thin skin of his fingertips
to prove he was brave.
He wore coke-bottle glasses,
tied his jacket around his neck
like a cape,
swore he was Superman.
"If you run fast enough,
you can fly," he said.

  At age 10, he died of cancer.
Mama told me it was his time.
"God collects his angels."

  I think of this boy every October,
if I should walk outside at twilight
into the smokehouse smell of burning leaves,
and suddenly a star falls.

  One Halloween he came to my door
asking "trick or treat"—
I kissed him.

  In dreams now, I take his hand
and we run as fast as we can
down the street past Mrs. Magregor's,
past the schoolyard's eerie silence,
our feet churning dust
till the wind catches our clothes, our hair,
and flings us in a rush at the sky.

The Missionary Writes to her Fiancé Concerning the Nature of Art

Dear David,

I read Chinese poetry
late at night
when everyone sleeps.
Li-Po laments the absence of his wife.
This is the point
where I should say how much I miss you,
compare myself to a lotus
and you the green-deep water on which I lie.
But spring comes.
Small birds with blue wings
flower in the trees
and each morning fills
with an ecstasy of sunshine.

Biography

Melissa Morphew is a graduate of the Ph.D. program in English at the University of Georgia where she won two Academy of American Poets Prizes. She is the 1994-95 recipient of an individual artist's grant from the Tennessee Arts Commission, and the winner of the 1993 Randall Jarrell International Poetry Prize.

Some of the magazines in which her work has appeared include: *Parnassus: Poetry in Review, Shenandoah, The Southern Poetry Review, Poetry East, Tar River Poetry, Poet Lore*, and *Spoon River Quarterly.* In 1995, Anabiosis Press published her chapbook *Hunger and Heat (The Missionary Letters).*

Ms. Morphew currently teaches at Morris College in Sumter, South Carolina.